Telling Tales
Stories in art

by Virginia Chandler

A+
Smart Apple Media

First published in 2005 by Hodder Wayland
338 Euston Road, London NW1 3BH, United Kingdom
Hodder Wayland is an imprint of Hodder Children's Books, a
division of Hodder Headline Limited.

This edition published under license from Hodder Children's
Books. All rights reserved.

Text copyright © Virginia Chandler 2005.

Series Concept: Ruth Thomson, Series Consultant: Erika
Langmuir, Editor and Picture Research: Margot Richardson,
Designers: Rachel Hamdi and Holly Mann

The publishers would like to thank the following for
permission to reproduce their pictures:
Page 1 © National Gallery Collection; 4–5 Bridgeman Art
Library/© The Detroit Institute of Arts; 6 Art Archive/Dagli Orti;
7 *left* Art Archive/Dagli Orti (A); 7 *right* Art Archive/Dagli Orti; 8
by special permission of the City of Bayeux;
9 © Hergé/Moulinsart 2004; 10–11 National Portrait Gallery
London; 12–13 Images/Victoria and Albert Museum;
14 © National Gallery Collection; by kind permission of the
Trustees of the National Gallery, London/CORBIS; 15 © The
Detroit Institute of Arts/The Bridgeman Art Library;
16–17 © Tate, London 2004; 18–19 © National Gallery
Collection; by kind permission of the Trustees of the National
Gallery, London/CORBIS; 20–21 Amon Carter Museum, Fort
Worth, Texas (1970.43); 22–23 Courtesy the Dorothea Lange
Collection, Oakland Museum of California; 24–25 © ADAGP,
Paris and DACS, London 2004, © Beatrice Soulé;
26–27 © Photo SCALA, Florence/Museum of Modern Art
(MoMA) New York © 2003, Digital image.

Published in the United States by Smart Apple Media
2140 Howard Drive West, North Mankato, Minnesota 56003

U.S. publication copyright © 2006 Smart Apple Media
International copyright reserved in all countries. No part of this
book may be reproduced in any form without written
permission from the publisher.
Printed in China

Library of Congress Cataloging-in-Publication Data

Chandler, Virginia.
Telling tales: stories in art / by Virginia Chandler.
p. cm. — (Artventure)
Includes index.
ISBN 1-58340-623-9
1. Narrative art—Juvenile literature. I. Title. II. Series.

N7433.93.C49 2005
709—dc22   2004059032

9 8 7 6 5 4 3 2 1

Contents

Words in **bold** can be found in the glossary

What's the story?

A story usually has a beginning, a middle, and an end—it is made up of events that happen over time. Artists who want to tell a story in their works have to solve a problem: how to get the storyline across through **still** images. The story may be from a well-known **legend** or history, or it may be invented by the artist.

The picture may show just one key moment or a whole series of events. But in every case, artists must use their skill to help the viewer "read" the picture—to recognize the main actors and understand what is going on.

❏ Benozzo Gozzoli, **Dance of Salome**, *1461/62*

A story sequence

One way to show the action unfolding is to bring together different **episodes** from a story in the same picture. The same characters may appear more than once.

Gozzoli used this idea to tell the Bible story of the death of John the Baptist. John had criticized King Herod and his new wife. She hated John and wanted revenge. Salome, her daughter, danced for Herod at a feast. He promised to give Salome whatever she wanted in return, so, to please her mother, she asked for the head of John on a dish.

Three in one

Gozzoli manages to show in one small picture three different scenes from this story. They take place at different times in the same palace. You might think the result would be confusing. But people of his day already knew this Bible story well, and he uses his art to make the **sequence** clear.

Dance of death

The central figure is the swirling Salome, dancing for King Herod at the feast. We follow her gaze to Herod. Look at Herod's expression. How does he feel about Salome's request—sad, eager, or worried? Herod's guests turn to him, wondering if Herod will keep his promise. How do we know the answer? (Clue: what is he holding in his hand?)

❑ Benozzo Gozzoli
Dance of Salome (detail)

Kneeling figures

Hidden from the party, to the left of the painting, John kneels while the executioner raises his sword. In an **alcove** at the rear, Salome appears again, kneeling. She places the dish with the gruesome head on her mother's lap.

In perspective

Gozzoli worked in Florence, Italy, in the 15th century. Artists then were studying the new science of **perspective**. They used its rules to draw scenes with a realistic feeling of depth and space. (If you follow the **diagonal** lines of the table, the walls, and the ceiling, you will see that they almost appear to meet at a central point.) Gozzoli uses perspective to divide and frame the different parts of the story.

A tall story

Some of the earliest stories told through art celebrate victory in war. Their main aim was to impress the viewer.

Trajan's triumph

The Roman emperor Trajan was a brilliant soldier. He won a series of victories in Dacia (today's Romania), returning to Rome with a huge amount of captured wealth. He used it to build a vast square, or **forum**, with magnificent public buildings to mark his triumph and the power of his empire.

A conquering hero

Towering over the forum was the marble column. It is carved with a **frieze**, which winds up like a long ribbon, recording the story of the conquest of Dacia. The story is told through clear and detailed images. The Roman army is shown marching, building camp, preparing food, and fighting—much as television news informs viewers today.

Trajan himself is the **focal point** of many scenes. He is shown as one of the men, rather than as a superhero, but the scale of his victory could not fail to impress the public.

❑ Unknown artists
Trajan's Column, Rome
Finished A.D. *113*
The column with its base is 125 feet (38 m) tall—about the height of a 12-story building.

The view at the top

Imagine you are in the small courtyard where the column then stood. Could you read the story all the way to the top? Even by standing on the roof of nearby buildings, it would be difficult to see it all.

- What different activities can you see in the building scene?
- How are the people dressed?
- Would a monument like this be built today? How are wars recorded and remembered now?

❏ Unknown artists, **Trajan's Column (detail)**
The Roman soldiers are building **fortifications**. Notice how the sculptor shifts from a frontal view to a "bird's-eye" view to show inside and outside the walls at the same time. It was important to make every detail clear.

❏ Unknown artists, **Trajan's Column (detail)**
On the upper band, soldiers build a camp. Notice, at the top left, one of the small, rectangular windows that let light in to the internal staircase. On the lower band, the giant river god looks on as the army sets out across a bridge of boats.

Why, then, record it in such rich detail? Perhaps one answer was found by climbing the inner staircase to the platform at the top. Looking down on the forum, the viewer would understand that it was these hard-fought Dacian wars that had brought such splendor to Rome.

Strip stories

A story can be told in a long band divided into segments. Each segment carries the action forward.

Embroidered history

The Bayeux **Tapestry** is a 230-foot (70 m) strip of linen **embroidered** with wool. It tells the story of the conquest of England in 1066 by William, the French Duke of Normandy. In this section, pillars divide the story into five **frames**.

A medieval movie

The story unfolds like a movie, with the action cutting from one storyline to another.

The Latin **captions**, as in a silent film, help identify people and places. Here, the key scene of Harold's coronation is like a still, or an official photograph. In the next two frames, the action is moved swiftly forward by using the same figures twice. They show that the coronation and the comet's warning are linked. The switch to an indoor scene takes the plot a step farther. The huddled, whispering figures deepen the feeling of danger and suspense.

❑ Unknown artists, **Bayeux Tapestry**
late 11th century
Odo, William's half brother and Bishop of Bayeux, had this made and hung in his cathedral in 1078 for everyone to see. It showed that William had a right to the English throne.

By special permission of the City of Bayeux

▲King Edward of England has died. He had promised the crown to his cousin William, but two noblemen are giving it to Harold.

▲Harold is crowned king by the Archbishop of Canterbury and sits on his throne.

▲Through an open door, five onlookers cheer for the new king.

▲They turn to point to an awesome sight in the sky: Halley's comet. It was thought to be an omen of disaster or war.

▲A messenger whispers to Harold. The ghostly ships in the border below hint at the fleet William is preparing for his invasion of England.

The clear line

Many of these storytelling techniques are found in modern cartoons 900 years later. In his books about the adventures of the fearless reporter Tintin, Belgian artist Hergé used what he called the "clear line," with simple drawing and flat, unshaded colors, to tell a story. Tintin has a round face with two points for eyes. Only his tuft of hair and baggy pants make him stand out.

Cartoon codes

Notice how, in this wordless scene, Hergé tells a lot through signs and marks.

• *Movement* is shown in frame one by the flying buckets and umbrella and the pose of the falling dog and startled Tintin. In frame three, short, repeated lines suggest the foot kicking the pipes.

❑ Hergé (Georges Remi)
The Calculus Affair (detail)
1956
Tintin and Captain Haddock are investigating a noise in the cellar when the dog, Snowy, tumbles down the stairs, knocking over some buckets.

• *Noises* are written in bold letters, with wavy sound lines.
• *Emotion* is shown through body language—notice Snowy's dazed expression and Tintin's urgent hands calling for quiet in frame two. His puzzled surprise is signaled by the question mark and beads of sweat above his head in frame three. The same marks above the prisoner's head show anger and stress.

• Do you think the Tapestry shares the "clear line" style? In what ways?

• What body language do the Tapestry figures use to make their feelings clear? Find someone who looks worried, confident, amazed.

A life story

Here, the events of one man's life are told in a single picture. Sir Henry Unton lived in England at the time of Queen Elizabeth I. When he died at the age of 40, Dorothy, his wife, ordered this painting to celebrate and record his life and learning.

❏ Unknown artist
The Life and Death of Sir Henry Unton
c. 1596

Follow the numbered captions to see the course of Unton's life, from birth to his grand funeral.

9 Dorothy kneels ▶ behind a statue of her husband on his magnificent tomb. It was really inside the church. Why has the artist shown it outside?

▲ **8** Henry was given an especially grand funeral because he died while serving the queen. Crowds of poor people watched the **somber** procession. What are they doing to get a good view?

6 Henry went as the queen's **ambassador** to France, where he fell ill. The French king's doctor looked after him.

4 He served as a soldier in the Low Countries (Belgium and the Netherlands). Where did the soldiers sleep?

- How many times does Sir Henry appear in the painting? How does the artist make him stand out?
- Imagine you are Dorothy talking about Henry. How would you describe him?

3 He traveled across the English Channel to Europe—first to Venice and Padua in Italy. What is he carrying and why?

2 The path leads to Oxford, where he studied. Can you spot him in his college room?

1 Baby Henry is in the arms of his mother. She was a countess, shown by her **coat of arms** and the coronet over her head.

Start here

7 Henry died, and his body was taken back to England by boat and horse-drawn cart.

5 These scenes show Henry's life at home: writing, playing music, talking to scholars, and enjoying a feast with friends.

A different angle on the story

By choosing to view a scene from an unusual **angle**, an artist can show separate threads of a story happening at the same time.

Small and detailed

This **miniature** is from a book that the great Akbar, Muslim emperor of northern India, had painted to illustrate his reign. It tells of the birth of his long-awaited first son and of the great joy of his **court** and people.

Indian painting at this time was famed for its exquisite and realistic detail. It was common for two or more artists to work together on such paintings. One might draw the **composition**, another the figures or heads, and another fill in the color.

Can you spot:
- a carpet of flowers?
- a boy on his father's shoulders?
- a peacock?
- a pair of cymbals?

Inside and out

Imagine you are standing next to the artist as he paints the scene. It is as though you are looking down on it from a high window whose frame cuts off parts of the palace and the figures. From where you are, you can see everything that is going on: the birth scene in the heart of the palace, the musicians celebrating in the courtyard, and the excited crowds gathering outside the walls. The angles of the palace form strong zigzag diagonals that separate the different scenes and, at the same time, lead the eye from one to the next.

❑ Kesu Salan and Dharmadas
The Birth of Prince Salim (detail)

Because of the high viewpoint, the sky and horizon are hardly visible. Notice the delicate painting of the rocks and river and the patterned palace tiles.

In the stillness of an inner room, Princess Padmi rests in bed while her maids gently wash the newborn baby.

Outside, by contrast, there is a noisy explosion of joy. Vividly dressed musicians are lifting their trumpets and beating drums. Another servant holds out a large dish of spiced rice to be given to the poor.

A courtier takes coins from a deep bag to throw over the wall to the people below.

Young and old, beggars, and holy men throng outside. They raise their arms to greet the new prince or to catch the coins. Notice how their gestures echo those of the musicians above them to form a great swirl of movement.

☐ Kesu Salan and Dharmadas
The Birth of Prince Salim
c. 1590

Moments of drama

An artist may choose a single dramatic moment to stand for the whole story. Such paintings usually illustrate a key point in a legend or Bible story that the audience of the time already knows well.

Sound and fury

Here, we are at the wedding feast of the Greek hero, Perseus, and Andromeda, whom he had rescued from a sea monster. The princess had once been promised to Phineas, who bursts into the scene with his men to kill Perseus and claim her. Perseus pulls out his secret weapon, the ghastly snake-haired head of Medusa, which turns all who look at it to stone. Giordano organizes the scene of **climax** so that we clearly know who is the hero, who is the villain, and what is going on.

- How does Medusa's head stand out?
- Why is Perseus turning his head away? How would you describe his expression?
- What is happening to Phineas and his men? (Clue: look at their skin color and poses.)
- What are the king and queen doing?

❏ Luca Giordano
Perseus Turning Phineas and His Followers to Stone
c. 1680
This huge painting measures 9 feet (2.75 m) by 12 feet (3.66 m). Compare this with the size of a wall in your home.

A Jewish heroine

This is also the story of a heroic act and a severed head—but the mood is very different. The Jewish heroine, Judith, saved her city from defeat by the Assyrian army. She and her servant tricked their way into the tent of the enemy general, Holofernes, and cut off his head while he slept. They carried his head back in a sack to prove that he was dead.

Deathly dark

In the darkness of the tent, Judith raises her hand as her servant stuffs the head into a sack. It is a moment of quiet but powerful suspense.

❏ Artemisia Gentileschi
Judith and Maidservant with the Head of Holofernes
c. 1625

• The women fill the canvas—they seem close to us. What feeling does that give you? Do they seem calm or afraid?

• Where is the light coming from? Where does it fall? The light casts deep shadows. What effect does this give?

A story full of clues

We sometimes have to do some detective work to read a picture. It can hold many clues that reveal the true story.

A moral tale

Like many artists in the 19th century, English painter Martineau chose subjects from everyday life to tell a tale and teach a lesson. The public enjoyed them much as people today enjoy television soap operas. To modern viewers, this painting seems at first to show a tired but happy family on moving day. But a viewer of the time would know how to find and recognize the signs that tell a different story.

❑ Robert Braithwaite Martineau, **The Last Day in the Old Home**, *1862*

A man of bad habits

Sir Charles Pulleyne has been forced to sell the family home and its contents to pay his debts. A painting of a racehorse, propped on the floor, shows he has gambled away his fortune at the races. Carefree and quite unashamed, he enjoys a last drink with his young son. He is clearly passing on his bad habits.

The ruined family

His wife stretches a tired hand in despair. But it is too late now to change his ways. Their old life, like the dying fire in the grate, has reached an end.

Find the hidden meaning in the details.
Why has Martineau shown:
- bare branches tapping at the window?
- the little girl holding her doll tightly?
- old family portraits on the walls?

Robert Braithwaite Martineau
The Last Day in the Old Home (details)

The family name

Behind the wineglass, the family's ancient coat of arms is carved on the fireplace. The father's drinking and fast living have blackened the family name.

A sad exchange

A tearful grandmother pays the butler his last wages, and he gives back the keys to the house. A newspaper advertises apartments for rent—a clue that the family's grand way of life is over.

Up for sale

All of the contents of the house are being removed for sale. A list of items lies on the carpet. Pictures and furniture are marked with white numbers. (Can you find them? There is one on the chair by the father's right knee.)

What's going to happen next?

❏ Joseph Wright of Derby
An Experiment on a Bird in the Air Pump
1768

Like any storyteller, an artist can use suspense to capture interest. Joseph Wright, an 18th-century English painter, lived in an age of great scientific discovery. He was friends with the leading thinkers and inventors of the day.

He went to meetings where experiments were carried out in front of an audience to explain the wonders and discoveries of science. It is just such a demonstration that he has chosen to paint here.

Life or death

A white cockatoo is in a glass jar attached to a pump. With one hand, the scientist pumps out the air. Unable to breathe, the bird falls. But with his left hand, the scientist holds the valve that can let air back into the flask to save the bird's life.

❏ Joseph Wright of Derby
An Experiment on a Bird in the Air Pump (detail)

It is truly a breathtaking moment. The scientist looks straight out of the picture at us, his eyebrows raised as though asking a question. Should he choose to carry on with the experiment or release the valve at the last minute? Will science or human kindness triumph? The face of the boy by the moonlit window also looks out at us. He holds a rope that will lower the cage so that the bird can be safely put back. Since a white cockatoo was a rare and precious bird, it was unlikely that the scientist would have killed it.

Mixed feelings

Their gazes draw us in to join the audience around the table. They are dramatically wrapped in darkness, with only the candlelight to reveal their faces and gestures. In this way, Wright focuses on their differing reactions to the experiment.

Read their expressions to see how young and old respond in different ways. Who is looking:
- fascinated?
- uninterested?
- thoughtful?
- afraid?

The two lovers on the left have eyes only for each other, while the boy next to them and the man timing the experiment with his watch pay close attention. A fatherly figure comforts the two frightened girls. The old man sits lost in thought, gazing at a skull in a glass jar on the table. He reminds us that this is a story not just of an experiment, but also of nature's laws of life and death.

A story within a story

When an artist tells more than one story in the same picture, the viewer may need help unraveling the puzzle.

❑ Grant Wood
Parson Weems' Fable
1939

An American legend

In 1806, Parson Weems wrote a life story of George Washington, the first president of the United States. He told how, as a boy, George had confessed to his father that he had chopped down a cherry tree.

His words, "I cannot tell a lie," became famous, and the story became a legend. George was held up as the model of a brave and honest young man. More than 100 years later, the American public was shocked to discover that Parson Weems had made up the story to glorify his hero. He was the one who had told a lie!

Setting the stage

Grant Wood was an American who painted in the early 20th century. He cleverly makes fun of *both* the inventive parson and his **fable** in one picture. Weems himself looks calmly out at us. He holds back a curtain to point at the cherry tree scene, as though it is happening on a stage. But Wood paints the tale with a new twist of his own. It is not quite the version the public loved. The storm clouds in the sky hint at something darker.

A little rebel

The red-faced, frowning father holds out an angry hand at George. George, in turn, points to the guilty ax but holds it out of his father's reach. He glares back, not at all sorry. Wood uses this play of hands and expressions in place of words. What do you think these two might be saying?

❑ Grant Wood
Parson Weems' Fable (detail)

Wood gives the little boy the head of the adult Washington as it is drawn on the American dollar bill. Why do you think he did this: so we can recognize him or to show that the great president was really a rebel? (Washington led the **War of Independence** against the British.)

The good son

The lines of the fallen tree, the lawn, and the house lead our eye to another cherry tree. A black slave shows more respect; he brings a ladder to help his mother pick fruit.

Notice Wood's storybook style and touches of humor.
• What is the fringe on the curtain made from?
• Where else can you see these round shapes repeated?
• What kinds of colors does Wood use for the main scene?

21

A news story

❏ Dorothea Lange
Migrant Mother, Nipomo, California
1936

Since the invention of photography, images of news stories from around the world have been able to reach our homes through newspapers and magazines. These pictures may have a greater impact than words.

The Great Depression

The early 1930s were a time of crisis in the U.S. Many Americans did not have jobs or homes. American photographer Dorothea Lange traveled around California, taking pictures of poor farm workers who had migrated there from other parts of the country to seek work. She used her photography to alert the government and the public to the hardships these people were facing.

Homeless and hungry

On her travels, Lange came across this **widowed** mother, Florence Owens, and her seven children, who were living in a tent in a pea-pickers' camp. The only things they had to eat were vegetables from the fields and birds the children killed. Lange later said of Owens, "She seemed to know my pictures might help her, and so she helped me. There was a sort of equality about it."

Lange took six photographs of the mother and her smallest children sitting in their makeshift tent, moving her camera in closer and closer to the scene. The other photographs show more details of their terrible living conditions. But this, the last picture in the series, is the most powerful.

- How would you describe the mother's expression? What might she be thinking?
- Why do you think the children's faces are turned away?
- Lange wanted her photographs of migrants to show "their pride, their strength, their spirit." Does she succeed here?
- Do you think the mother is brave or defeated?

Close up

The mother holds her baby while the others huddle around her for comfort. The camera is so close that we can see the rough texture of their shabby, grimy clothes. Owens was only 32 years old, yet she looks much older. Her face is weather-beaten and lined with worry. The thin, tense hand raised to her mouth and the haunting expression in her eyes reveal the misery of the migrant's life.

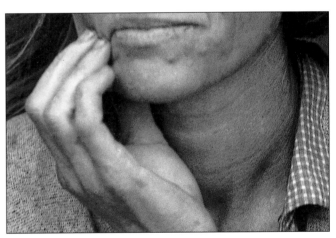

☐ Dorothea Lange, **Migrant Mother, Nipomo, California (detail)**
What does this gesture tell about the mother's feelings?

A call for help

When Lange's photos of the family were published in the *San Francisco News*, the country was deeply shocked. The government immediately sent food aid for the starving workers. This portrait came to sum up the story of the **Depression**.

Stories in the round

A story retold in sculpture can be especially vivid. Moving around the figures, seeing them from all sides, we can enter into their drama.

From Western to legend

Senegalese sculptor Ousmane Sow has re-created the Battle of Little Big Horn of 1876, in which the **Native Americans**, led by Sitting Bull, defeated General Custer's Seventh Cavalry.

In a panorama of 24 larger-than-life figures and 11 horses, the two sides charge and fall, fight and flee. All of the terrible drama of the battlefield is there. However, Sow has not simply created a sculpted Western film with its "goodies" and "baddies." He sees a link between the Native Americans and his fellow Africans, who suffered as slaves at the hands of the white man. The battle becomes part of a bigger story.

❏ Ousmane Sow
The Battle of Little Big Horn—The Charge of Two Moon
1998
In this group of sculptures, Cheyenne Chief Two Moon looms over two fallen soldiers and a tangle of dead horses.

Sow worked for many years as a physiotherapist, healing through massage. His expert knowledge and touch bring to life the veins and muscles of the chief's strong arm and body. Sow's unusual training and technique help to make his sculptures very expressive.

Each sculpture starts with a frame of metal and wires, which Sow builds on with cloth and fibers and then covers with a homemade paste of glue, resin, and secret ingredients.

• Can you see where the different materials are visible?

• What textures do the sculptures have?

• What kinds of colors does Sow use? Compare them with the Senegal landscape where the sculptures were photographed.

❏ Ousmane Sow, **The Battle of Little Big Horn—The Charge of Two Moon (detail)**

Although Little Big Horn brought the death of Custer and victory for the Native Americans, Sow does not show it as a triumph. The bodies of the fallen soldiers are twisted with pain and fear, but we do not see blood or wounds. The pointless tragedy of war is expressed in the tangled bodies of the magnificent horses. Above them, Chief Two Moon looks down.

With his powerful, muscled body and noble head, he is like a hero in a legend. His face does not show hatred or anger. Instead, he has an expression of great dignity and sadness. It is as if he knows that the victory will be short-lived: 14 years later, the Native Americans would be defeated at the Battle of Wounded Knee.

You tell the story

Artists can create adventures in dreamed or imagined worlds that would be difficult to express with words. Their poetic images invite us to invent stories of our own.

Rousseau was a self-taught French painter. He showed his work at the annual Paris show of artists, which accepted pictures by painters like himself. He was mocked for his simple vision but still believed that he was a great artist. Rousseau drew from nature, botanical gardens, or the zoo. He combined the reality of what he saw with the equally vivid world of his imagination. This gives a dreamlike feeling to his paintings.

A mysterious vision

This painting captures the innocence and strangeness of Rousseau's vision. The gypsy, the lion, the jug, and the mandolin are all objects from the real world. Set together in this timeless, other-worldly landscape, they become mysterious. What are they doing here? The gypsy's body and the waving stripes of her rainbow-colored robe follow the contours of the desert sand. The lion stands out against the night sky like a statue. There is an atmosphere of eerie stillness.

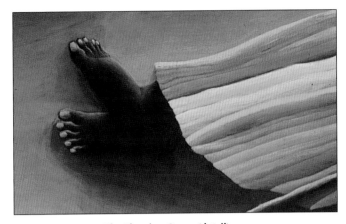

❏ Henri Rousseau, **The Sleeping Gypsy (detail)**

Dream world

Rousseau uses smooth, careful brushwork and pays great attention to details such as the lion's mane and the gypsy's delicately painted feet—which shows his close observation of **reality**. But in some ways, the scene is very unreal. Look at the odd way the gypsy and the mandolin are tilted toward the viewer and the way the background is flattened like a stage set.

- Do you think the lion is real or part of the gypsy's dream?
- Does the lion look fierce or friendly?
- Is the light harsh or soft? Where does it come from?
- What details catch the light?
- Imagine the gypsy's story. What do you think will happen next?

❏ Henri Rousseau, **The Sleeping Gypsy (detail)**

About the artists

The symbols below show the size and shape of the works shown in this book compared with an average-sized adult.

Artemisia GENTILESCHI (page 15)

(1593–1652) Italian (Rome)
Judith and Maidservant with the Head of Holofernes, c. 1625
Oil on canvas, 72.5 x 55.7 inches (184.1 x 141.6 cm)
© Detroit Institute of Arts, Michigan

Other works

❏ *Judith Beheading Holofernes*, 1618
   Uffizi Gallery, Florence, Italy
❏ *Esther before Ahasuerus*, 1628–35
   Metropolitan Museum of Art, New York
❏ *Self-portrait as the Allegory of Painting*, 1630s
   Kensington Palace, London, UK

Luca GIORDANO (page 14)

(1634–1705) Italian (Naples)
Perseus Turning Phineas and His Followers to Stone, c. 1680
Oil on canvas,
108.3 x 144 inches (275 x 366 cm)
National Gallery, London, UK

Other works

❏ *The Allegory of the Golden Fleece*, 1697
   Prado, Madrid, Spain
❏ *The Fall of the Rebel Angels*, 1666
   Kunsthistorisches Musem, Vienna, Austria
❏ *Diana and Endymion*, 1675/80
   National Gallery of Art, Washington, D.C.

Benozzo di Lese di Sandro GOZZOLI (pages 4–5)

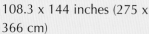

(c. 1420–97) Italian (Florence)
Dance of Salome, 1461/62
Tempera on panel, 9.4 x 13.6 inches (23.8 x 34.5 cm)
National Gallery of Art, Washington, D.C.

Other works

❏ *The Procession of the Three Kings*, 1459
   Medici Chapel, Palazzo Riccardi, Florence, Italy
❏ *St. Peter and Simon the Magus*
   Metropolitan Museum of Art, New York
❏ *The City of Babylon*, 1468–84
   Camposanto, Pisa, Italy

Hergé (Georges REMI) (page 9)

(1907–83) Belgian (Brussels)
The Calculus Affair, detail, page 25
Artwork © 1956, 1984 Casterman, text © 1960
Methuen Children's Books 1973 (English version)

Other works

❏ *The Black Island*, 1938, English version 1966
❏ *Tintin in America*, 1932, English version 1978

KESU SALAN and DHARMADAS (pages 12–13)

(second half 16th century) Indian. Painters of the Court of Emperor Akbar.
The Birth of Prince Salim, c. 1590
Watercolor on paper, 12.6 x 7.4 inches (32 x 18.9 cm)
Victoria and Albert Museum, London, UK

Dorothea LANGE (pages 22–23)

(1895–1965) American (New Jersey)
Migrant Mother, Nipomo, California, 1936
(Full title: Destitute pea-pickers in California;
a 32 year old mother of seven children. February 1936)
Photograph (gelatin silver print),
approx. 13.4 x 10.6 inches (34 x 27 cm)
Oakland Museum, California

Other works

❑ *Jobless on edge of pea field,* 1937
   J. Paul Getty Museum, Los Angeles, California
❑ *White Angel bread line,* 1933
   George Eastman House, Rochester, New York
❑ *Cotton picker, Eloy,* 1940
   Metropolitan Museum of Art, New York

Robert Braithwaite MARTINEAU
(pages 16–17)

(1826–1869) English (London)
The Last Day in the Old Home, 1862
Oil on canvas, 42.2 x 57 inches (107.3 x 144.8 cm)
Tate Gallery, London, UK

Other works

❑ *Kit's First Writing Lesson,* 1852
   Tate Gallery, London, UK
❑ *The Last Chapter,* 1863
   Birmingham City Art Gallery and Museum, UK
❑ *Katherine and Petruchio,* 1855
   Ashmolean Museum, Oxford, UK

Henri ROUSSEAU (pages 26–27)

(1844–1910) French (Lavel)
The Sleeping Gypsy, 1897
Oil on canvas, 51 x 79 inches (129.5 x 200.7 cm)
Museum of Modern Art, New York

Other works

❑ *War,* 1894
   Musée du Louvre, Paris, France
❑ *Tropical Forest with Monkeys,* 1910
   National Gallery of Art, Washington, D.C.
❑ *Yadwiga's Dream,* 1910
   Museum of Modern Art, New York

Ousmane SOW (pages 24–25)

(1935–) Senegalese (Dakar)
The Battle of Little
Big Horn, 1998
Mixed media,
group of 24 figures
and 11 horses, slightly larger than life-size
Collection of the artist

Other works

❑ *The Runner on the Starting Line,* 2001
   Headquarters of Olympic Games Committee,
   Lausanne, Switzerland
❑ *Reclining Nouba,* 1984
   Museum of Troyes, France
❑ *The Wrestlers,* 1984
   Les Abattoirs Modern Art Museum, Toulouse, France

Grant WOOD (pages 20–21)

(1891–1942) American (Iowa)
Parson Weems' Fable, 1939
Oil on canvas, 38.4 x 50.1 inches (97.5 x 127.3 cm)
Amon Carter Museum, Fort Worth, Texas (1970.43)

Other works

❏ *American Gothic*, 1930
    Art Institute of Chicago, Illinois
❏ *Midnight Ride of Paul Revere*, 1931
    Metropolitan Museum of Art, New York
❏ *Death on the Ridge Road*, 1935
    Williams College Museum of Art, Massachusetts

Joseph WRIGHT of Derby (pages 18–19)

(1734–97) English (Derby)
An Experiment on a Bird in the Air Pump, 1768
Oil on canvas, 72 x 96.1 inches (183 x 244 cm)
National Gallery, London, UK

Other works

❏ *A Philosopher Lecturing with a Mechanical Planetary*, 1766
    Derby Museum and Art Gallery, Derby, UK
❏ *The Blacksmith's Shop*, 1771
    Yale Center for British Art, New Haven, Connecticut
❏ *An Eruption of Vesuvius*, 1774–76
    The Huntington, San Marino, California

Unknown artists (pages 6–7)

Trajan's Column, Finished A.D. 113
Marble, height 98 feet (29.77 m),
(125 feet, or 38 m, with pedestal),
diameter 12 feet (3.7 m)
Trajan's Forum, Rome, Italy

Unknown artists (page 8)

The Bayeux Tapestry (detail),
late 11th century
Linen embroidered in wool,
19.7 inches x 230 feet (50 cm x 70 m)
William the Conquerer Center, Bayeux, France

Unknown artist (pages 10–11)

The Life and Death of Sir Henry Unton,
c. 1596
Oil on panel, 29.1 x 64.3 inches (74 x 163.2 cm)
National Portrait Gallery, London, UK

Glossary

Alcove A small space set back in a wall.

Ambassador A person who represents his country or ruler in another country.

Angle A position from which something is viewed.

Captions Titles or brief explanations added to pictures or cartoons.

Climax The most intense, exciting, or important point of something.

Coat of arms A shield with symbols or pictures on it that is unique to a person, family, or country.

Composition The organization of the parts of a picture.

Court The people who live with and/or work for a ruler such as a king or queen.

Depression A slump or downturn in the economy of a country during which many people cannot find work. The Great Depression of the 1930s affected many countries around the world.

Diagonal Having a slanted direction.

Embroidered Sewn with thread or yarn to make patterns or pictures.

Episodes A group of events that form part of a sequence.

Fable A story not based on fact, often with a moral message.

Focal point The center of interest or activity.

Fortifications Buildings or walls that are built to prevent an attack.

Forum A square or marketplace in an ancient Roman city, used for meetings and business.

Frame A single complete picture in a series of pictures.

Frieze A broad band of sculpture or painting.

Legend A story that comes from history but that may not be true.

Miniature A small-scale, minutely finished painting.

Native Americans A native person from America. Also sometimes called an American Indian.

Perspective A method of painting or drawing landscapes, figures, and objects to make them appear three-dimensional.

Reality What really exists, rather than what is imagined.

Sequence A particular order in which pictures or events follow each other.

Somber Dark or gloomy.

Still A photograph or a single shot from a film.

Tapestry Fabric with a design woven into it or stitched onto it.

War of Independence A war fought by the American colonies to win their independence from Great Britain (1775-83).

Widowed Became a widow (woman) or widower (man) because a husband or wife died.

Index

Numbers in **bold** show page numbers of illustrations